Get in the Game! With Robin Roberts

Which Sport Is RIGHT For You?

The Millbrook Press   Brookfield, Connecticut

The author and publisher wish to thank
Bill Gutman for his research and writing
contributions to this series.

Published by The Millbrook Press, Inc.
2 Old New Milford Road
Brookfield, Connecticut 06804
www.millbrookpress.com

Cover photograph courtesy of Steve Fenn/ABC
Photographs courtesy of © Patrick Flynn: p. 4;
SportsChrome USA: p. 6 (left © Steve
Woltmann); Icon SMI: pp. 6 (right © John
Cordes), 13 (© Robert Beck); Photo Researchers,
Inc.: pp. 11 (© Tim Davis), 16 (top © B. Seitz);
Corbis: pp. 16 (bottom © James Marshall), 17
(top © Richard T. Nowitz), 29 (© AFP), 38;
PhotoEdit: pp. 17 (bottom © Tony Freeman), 18
(© Michael Newman), 36 (© David Young-Wolff);
Allsport: p. 24 (© Michael Steele); AP/Wide
World Photos: p. 31

Library of Congress Cataloging-in-Publication
Data
Roberts, Robin, 1960-
Which sport is right for you?
p. cm. — (Get in the game! With Robin Roberts)
Includes index.
ISBN 0-7613-2117-9 (lib. bdg.). — 0-7613-1475-x (pbk)
1. Sports for girls—Juvenile literature. 2. Sports—
Psychological aspects—Juvenile literature.
[1. Sports for women.] I. Title.
GV709 .R64 2001 796'.083'42—dc21 00-069193

CONTENTS

Introduction

Sports has always been a big part of my life. From playing sandlot football with the other kids in my neighborhood in Biloxi, Mississippi, to playing tennis in high school and basketball in college, to working in sports broadcasting at ESPN, I can't imagine my life without sports. It used to be that girls who played sports were labeled "tomboys." These days, however, women and sports go hand-in-hand in so many ways.

Sports can increase a girl's confidence and help her to feel good about herself, and can help her succeed in nearly every aspect of life including school, a career, and relationships with friends and family.

With **Get in the Game!** my goal is to share my love and knowledge of the world of sports, and to show just how important sports can be. What you can learn on the field, court, rink, and arena are ways to solve problems, communicate with others, and become a leader. No matter what your skill level, if you learn all that sports can teach you, how can you *not* succeed at life in general? And the best part is that, like I have, you'll have fun at the same time!

—Robin Roberts

One thing to consider when thinking about which sport is right for you is whether you want to play a team sport such as volleyball, an individual sport like golf, or a combination of the two.

What is it about sports that excites you the most? Is it crossing the finish line first in the 100-meter dash? Is it drilling a long jump shot at a crucial point in a game? Perhaps you most enjoy diving to make a save as the soccer ball is headed to the net. Then again, your favorite sports moment may come when you leap high in the air to slam a volleyball past the reach of your opponents, or maybe it's executing a perfect maneuver on the balance beam.

Almost everyone who plays sports will eventually find one activity that she likes better than the others, and maybe even one or two aspects of that sport that give her the most satisfaction. For a young athlete, however, finding "the" sport and the magical feeling it can produce isn't always an easy thing.

In days past, it was mostly boys who were playing sports. Those growing up and playing in the United States usually chose from baseball, football, and basketball. There were other sports, of course, but the majority of young athletes participated in the so-called big three. But times have changed. Not only are there nearly as many girls participating in sports as boys, but there are also many more popular sports from which to choose.

With sports playing such a major role in today's world and in the life of so many youngsters, there is yet another new phenomenon: the sports specialist. The theory is that if an athlete really wants to become good at a sport, she should choose one early on and concentrate on it to the exclusion of all the other sports.

This brings two questions to mind: How do you find the one sport that is right for you? And, even more important, is one sport a good thing?

This book will look into these questions. If you have a love of sports you will probably begin searching for the ones you enjoy the most and can play the best. If you want to try a new sport, what skills will you need and how do you know if you have them? What if you really love playing one sport, but are better at another that you don't like as much? What if you love two or three sports, but your parents and coaches want you to give up all but your best one?

Sports are fun and healthful activities that will give you self-confidence, a sense of achievement, the ability to work with others, and, if you play a team sport, the camaraderie that comes with being part of a team. Finding the sport or sports best suited to your talents, interests, and personality will only add to the benefits that they can bring to your life.

When Is the Best Time to Begin?

According to recent statistics, there are more than 20 million American children involved in some type of out-of-school sports programs throughout the country. Many of these children are learning the skills of a sport for the first time. Others play more than one sport, while still others have picked a single sport at which they are working to excel.

In all of these scenarios, sports should be part of a healthy lifestyle that will benefit a young athlete in many ways. Jean Zimmerman and Gil Reavill, authors of *Raising Our Athletic Daughters*, were asked how participating in sports helps young girls. This is what they said.

"Girls who participate in sports are less likely to drop out of school, more likely to go on to college, and more likely to graduate from college. They tend to avoid a whole host of risk-taking and self-destructive behaviors. [Female] athletes have one of the lowest rates of tobacco use among any sector of the high-school population; [and] they are less likely to abuse drugs . . . than girls who do not participate in sports."

The authors went on to say that girls who are involved in athletics have more confidence and self-esteem, have a more positive image of their bodies, and are, on the whole, achievers with a strong sense of focus.

There is no argument about the ultimate value of sports in the life of every young person. That makes it even more important for you to get the right kind of sports background and make the right choices as you grow older. Knowing about early sports development in children will help you see if you are moving in the right direction.

Children as young as two or three years old can begin learning motor

Little girls can learn the skills necessary to enjoy activities such as roller blading, and these can help them master other sports skills later.

skills such as catching, falling, run-
ning, hopping, and skipping. At
three and four, youngsters don't
have the attention span or ability to
understand the rules of complex
sports, but at that age they are able
to enjoy a few individual activities,
such as swimming and tumbling.

Authors Zimmerman and Reavill
offer another piece of advice for girls
of this age. Many boys at the age of
three or four have already been
exposed to throwing and catching.
Traditionally, girls have not had this
exposure—they have been directed
to other, nonsports activities.

"By kindergarten," the authors
said, "boys tend to be further along
the athletic skill-level spectrum than
their girl peers. . . . We tend not to
give girls the basic tools they need to
have a successful sports experience.

"The most important thing that
parents can do is . . . teach a girl

how to throw overhand. The overhand throw is the basis for so many
sports activities — baseball . . . the
tennis serve, the volleyball serve
and spike, the forward pass in football, even the javelin throw. It
should be 'equipment' for all little
girls growing up."

Kids can begin to develop other
basic sports skills at about age six.
At this point, experts suggest they
choose sports that help develop
hand-eye coordination, agility,
strength, and muscular coordination. Examples of sports that rein-
force these skills are T-ball, soccer,
gymnastics, swimming, cycling,
skating, and other noncontact
sports.

When girls are between eight
and ten years old, they can begin
contact sports. At this age you will
be able to understand your role in
team sports as well as the complex

The overhand throw is a sports skill that is often taught to boys more than it is taught to girls. Yet it's a basic skill a girl will need in many of the sports she participates in.

rules of the game. This is the time to begin sports such as basketball, softball, wrestling, and volleyball. There is, however, a difference between contact and collision sports, such as football or hockey. These are generally not recommended for children under the age of ten.

Always begin a new sport slowly. Learn the basic skills. If you like sports, but no one in your home plays, ask your parents to find a place where you can learn. It may be at school, a community center, or church. It may be with others in your neighborhood. Take your time. Watch sports you think you may like. Learn some of the skills. Talk to your friends who play. Then, if you like what you see and hear, try it.

Should I Play a Team Sport or an Individual Sport?

One of the most important things to consider when looking for a sport is whether you want to play a team sport or an individual sport. There certainly isn't any law against playing both kinds. In fact, some athletes find they like the change from a team to an individual sport from time to time.

In a team sport, you are part of a group of athletes all striving for the same thing: You want your team to play the best it possibly can and hopefully win the game. That means putting the team ahead of your own individual accomplishments. You must learn to get along with your teammates and work with them on the field or court. If you play only for yourself and ignore your teammates, you risk hurting the team.

In basketball, the five teammates on the court must work together on both offense and defense. Maybe you are a great jump shooter. You get the ball beyond the three-point arc near the end of a close game. You know if you hit the shot, you will have scored more than 20 points for the game. At the same time, however, you see a teammate cutting toward the basket with a defensive player behind her. If you are not a team player, you would ignore your teammate and take the jump shot because you want those 20 points. If you are a team player, you would pass the ball in this situation, because you know that the short layup your teammate under the basket can make is more likely to go in than your long jump shot. This is what is meant by putting the team ahead of yourself.

A good team player can achieve both team and individual goals. She can help her team to win while

Team or individual sport?

Soccer and softball are team sports. And while swimmers or runners might be part of a larger team, these are considered individual sports since performance depends on a single athlete.

becoming the best player she can be. To be a good team player, you must be unselfish. You must be willing to make sacrifices. Part of your goal must be to help make your teammates better players. You can't worry about how many points you score, how many hits you get, or whether you score the winning goal. If the team wins, you win. If everyone plays well and plays together, but the team loses, its players are still winners. Other team sports include softball, volleyball, field hockey, soccer, and ice hockey.

By contrast, in an individual sport, for the most part, you have to be concerned only about your own performance. The challenge is to keep improving. If you are a runner, you want to finish first and improve your time. If you are a tennis player, you want to win the match, but also

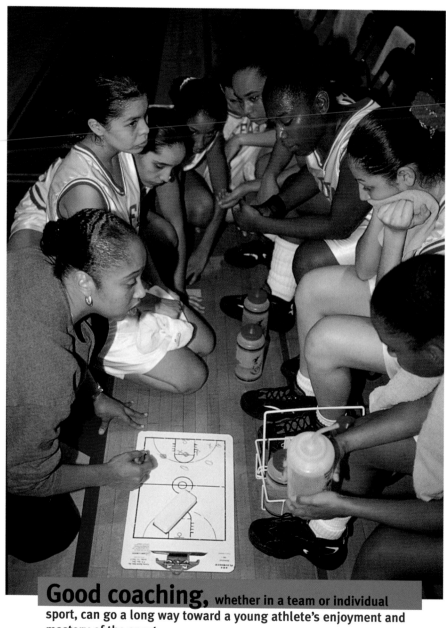

Good coaching, whether in a team or individual sport, can go a long way toward a young athlete's enjoyment and mastery of the sport.

make sure that your skills continue to get better. If you love swimming, you must keep yourself in topflight condition and try to get a new personal best time in your event each time you compete. In other words, you must constantly challenge and motivate yourself to improve.

In some ways, you can also be involved in an individual sport and still be part of a team. For example, when you swim against competition, you are competing for yourself in that individual race. At the same time, you may be part of a swimming team and, by winning your event, help the team to get points. In this situation, you have the experience of competing in an individual event, but also the camaraderie of interacting with teammates. Other individual sports are tennis, golf, track and field, gymnastics, rowing, martial arts, and figure skating.

How do you decide if you are better suited for a team sport or an individual sport? It helps to think about the kind of person you are and some of the other things you enjoy doing. For example, if you enjoy being with a group of friends, sharing things with them, and doing things together, a team sport might be right for you. If, however, you tend to want to do things by yourself, spend time alone, and not have too many people tell you what to do, then an individual sport might work better for you.

Another thing to consider is whether you make friends easily and can get along with different types of people. As a member of a sports team, you will have new teammates all the time. Each one can't be your best friend. However, you must get along to work well with them during practices and games. By contrast, if you are shy and hold back from making new friends, perhaps you should begin your sports career with an individual sport. You can always move into a team sport once you have built more confidence.

One more thing to consider is how well you accept an older person telling you what to do. Ask yourself if you occasionally resent your parents when they tell you to do something you might not want to do just then. Do you mope a bit, not move as quickly as they would like? If that's the case, you may also have trouble taking orders from a coach. Coaches in both team and individual sports are going to tell you what to do—that is their job. Some will give orders in a harsher way than others. But every coach expects you to take criticism, to learn the lessons she is teaching, and to allow her to direct you during a game or a competition.

Outstanding coaches can be a blessing. They can teach you about a sport, and also how to apply the lessons learned to other areas of your life. They will listen to your questions and try to explain the things you might not agree with at first. Other coaches are more demanding. They feel they are in charge and shouldn't be questioned. If you play sports long enough, you will probably meet both kinds. So whether you choose a team or individual sport, you must be able to follow the coach's lead and make the best of the situation in which you are competing. Working within the context of a team takes a good degree of maturity. If you don't feel you are ready for the responsibility of being part of a team, or you might have trouble cooperating with others in the group, then you might enjoy an individual sport more.

This isn't an easy choice, especially at the beginning of your athletic career. There are many exciting team and individual sports for you to play. Chances are you will want to try a number of them. If you start with a team sport, you can still move on to an individual one, and vice versa. Before you start, however, think about the kind of person you are, what kinds of sports you might like, and where you feel you will fit best.

How Many Sports Should I Play?

Sports are fun. That should be the first thing you think about when choosing and playing a sport, and then moving on to play others. Have fun while you are learning the skills of a new sport, including working with teammates, making new friends, and learning to take instruction and sometimes criticism from a coach. Sometimes learning to play a sport isn't easy. Sometimes it can lead to periods of frustration, as well as bumps and bruises. Therefore, it's certainly better if, overall, you are enjoying it and having fun.

When learning new sports, a young athlete often begins to wonder how many sports she should play? Should she concentrate on just one, her best sport, or play a variety? Sports doctor Edward R. Laskowski, M.D., Minnesota, feels it is important for youngsters to play a variety of sports.

"If children develop good foundational skills — rather than specializing in a sport — they likely will be able to succeed at a wider variety of sports and activities during their lifetimes," Dr. Laskowski explained.

Coaches and other observers of the youth sports scene also find that youngsters' tastes tend to change frequently as they grow and mature. At age eight, a girl might say that soccer is the right sport for her. A year later, she might prefer volleyball. Two years after that, she might decide she wants to be a great basketball player. A year later, she might decide that she loves swimming better than all the others. Why not try all of them before deciding on a favorite?

Marion Jones, the great sprinter who won three gold medals at the 2000 Summer Olympic Games, grew up as an all-around athlete playing numerous sports. By the time she reached high school she was outstanding in both basketball and track. Because she loved both sports, she didn't want to choose one and give up the other. When she entered the University of North Carolina, she made it clear that she was going to compete in both sports.

"I love track," she said, "and I wanted to keep it like that. So many young runners get burned out. I figured I'd do both. . . . I [felt I] needed discipline, and the Carolina basketball program was very structured." Marion sensed she could get something positive from both sports. She enjoyed being part of a team and working together for a common goal. She said she loved playing

To reach her goal
of winning Olympic medals in track and field, Marion Jones chose to focus on that one sport.

alongside women who were skilled and competitive.

Even though many felt she could have gone on to a professional basketball career in the WNBA, Marion finally set a goal of winning Olympic medals in track. Once her ultimate goal was set, she devoted all of her time to that sport. Yet even her track coach, Trevor Graham, admitted that Marion's basketball experience benefitted her track career: "She had become more explosive and aggressive on the track because of basketball."

In addition, there was no burnout. She was able to concentrate on track and her Olympic goals with a renewed love for the sport. Though it wasn't always easy, competing in two sports at an elite level for a while was the best choice for Marion Jones.

If you want to play more than one sport, how many should you play? Taking this approach, can you find yourself playing too many different sports? Remember the first three words of this chapter. Sports are fun! If you find yourself getting tired of playing one sport, move on to another. Sometimes playing a variety of sports can keep you interested and make each new season exciting all over again.

However, if you are playing so many different sports that you have time for little else, then you may be overdoing it. Today, there are more sports programs than ever, both in and out of school. Kids can start as young as three years old. They can play multiple sports in one season or one sport all year round. There are summer sports camps to fit the needs of nearly every young athlete.

As author Jonathan Buzby put it in his article *Preventing Burnout in Youth Sports*: "The best aspect of youth sports . . . may also be the most troubling aspect."

What he means is that there are so many sports opportunities that some kids are actually overdoing it. They are playing too many sports without rest or they are playing one sport all the time without rest. Neither is a good idea. The result of too much sports activity can be injuries or burnout. Since it is your decision what sports to play and how much time to spend playing, you should be aware of the signs of burnout.

If the fun of sports stops, for example, you might be doing too much. If you begin to feel tired and run-down instead of healthy and invigorated, you might be playing too much. If you are not getting your schoolwork done, and have no time to spend with friends and family outside of your sport, then you are spending too much time with it. And if you suddenly feel like quitting, then you know you are in danger of burning out.

How, then, do you strike a balance, especially if you love playing? For starters, try the sports you think you would like. Don't let anyone tell you that you can't play a sport—that you are too short, too slow, or not strong enough.

If it's an individual sport such as gymnastics, you will need a coach to teach you how to perform the various maneuvers safely. If it's a team sport such as soccer or basketball, you can start by playing with your friends and then find a program within your town or school.

Sometimes you might try three or four sports before you find the one you like best. Perhaps the one you like best won't be the one you play best. Do you just want to have fun playing your favorite sport, do you want to play the sport you are best at to see how good you can become, or do you want to do both?

You can also try alternating very different sports. If you have a tough soccer season where there is some physical contact and hard falls, you can try an individual sport such as swimming or tennis where there is no contact and fewer falls and tumbles.

Remember that growing bodies need time to build. When you play a sport, the muscles that you use develop small tears. This is a natural process. Then when you rest, the muscles heal and become stronger. Make sure you have time for rest and other activities in your life. And when you do play, work hard, listen to your coach, try to improve your game, and keep having fun!

Should I Ever Pick Just One Sport?

There is often tremendous pressure on young athletes to excel. Even a nine- or ten-year-old athlete who is the best among her peers can bring tremendous satisfaction and a sense of pride to her parents, coaches, and peers. She is often treated the same way as a great professional athlete — as a star. Those around her often see her as the next Mia Hamm, Marion Jones, Venus Williams, Sheryl Swoopes, or Lisa Fernandez. Sometimes she is told that many times over.

Those who support the cause of kids concentrating on a single sport will point to examples such as Tiger Woods and the Williams sisters, Venus and Serena. Woods was swinging a golf club as soon as he could walk and was considered a phenom by the time he was five years old. Today, he is the best golfer in the world and in the eyes of many, on his way to becoming the best of all time.

Both Venus and Serena Williams were hitting tennis balls before they were five years old. It was their only sport. Today, they are both tennis champions. Their power and athleticism has revolutionized the women's game. Like Tiger Woods, they have the potential to become among the best ever. Amazing athletes like these are a joy to watch and an inspiration to young people. But sometimes athletes, parents, and coaches need to remember that in the real world, not everyone can be a Woods or a Williams.

In fact, the pressure to play and excel at one sport often comes more

Tennis superstars
Venus and Serena Williams

from parents than from the young athlete herself. Rick Wolff, a sports psychologist and author of *Coaching Kids for Dummies,* confirmed this theory. "[Their kids] excelling in sports has become just as much a part of the American dream for parents as getting their kids into the best schools and living in the best neighborhoods."

When you excel at a sport at an early age, you're often told that to maximize your potential, you should concentrate on that sport to the exclusion of all others. If you play more than one, you are told, it will take time away from your development in your best sport. There are literally thousands of programs around the country that enable kids to play one sport all year round.

Some kids are motivated by their athletic heroes. They feel they can make their own mark in a pro-

fessional sport someday, but to do that they must work at only that sport. But parents and kids who feel that sports is a ticket to a college scholarship are pinning their hopes against some steep odds. Statistics show that less than one percent of kids playing organized sports will receive a college athletic scholarship.

While a few young athletes might benefit from becoming specialists at an early age, chances are the majority will not fare well for a variety of reasons.

First and foremost is the matter of a young athlete's physical health. As mentioned earlier, it is a medical fact that playing the same sport for months on end can cause excessive stress to the same part of the body. This can lead to overuse injuries such as tendinitis and stress fractures.

This statement from the American Academy of Pediatrics (AAP), formed after long and careful study, makes this abundantly clear: "Research supports the recommendation that child athletes avoid early sports specialization. Those who participate in a variety of sports and specialize only after reaching the age of puberty tend to be more consistent performers, have fewer injuries and adhere to sports play longer than those who specialize early."

If you are playing one sport all year round, practicing without a break, you might also find some

Athletes like the **Williams sisters** and champion figure skater **Michelle Kwan** are an inspiration to young people. But unless a young athlete has outstanding natural ability in one sport, it is usually recommended that she play a variety of sports.

other signs of trouble. Are you losing weight, feeling tired all the time, or having trouble keeping up your grades at school? If you are experiencing any of these symptoms, you might be working too hard at your sport. This can also happen, of course, if you are going from one sport to another throughout the year with no rest. But playing a variety of sports can sometimes reenergize you.

Yet sometimes there is pressure from sports leagues, coaches, and parents for top athletes to specialize early. There have been instances of various programs and coaches discouraging participants from playing other sports.

One case involved an article that listed other sports that might hurt a young player's tennis game. It suggested strongly that those working hard at tennis refrain from playing baseball or softball. In effect, the article claimed that swinging a bat in baseball or softball would have a bad effect on the tennis stroke. Returning from playing ball, it said, young tennis players tended to "hit home runs" on the tennis court to raise their racquets too high on their backswing, and to have trouble keeping the swings of the two sports separated.

But what happens to the young tennis player whose friends want to go out and play softball on a Saturday afternoon? Does she say her tennis coach or parents won't let her, and miss out on a good time with her friends? Does she play and hope her tennis game won't suffer? Or does she sit and watch, wishing she could play, starting to resent the fact that she's so good at tennis that she can't have fun with softball? It's not an easy choice for a young athlete to make.

Kids who focus on one sport early, not only play year round, but often play in two or more leagues at the same time. The so-called elite leagues often travel far from home to play other elite teams. Sometimes the entire family must be involved, taking their young athlete to games and practices, traveling to watch them play, sacrificing parts of their own lives. With this kind of time invested, parents are often satisfied only when their child is the star and the team wins. If the child isn't doing as well as expected, the parents sometimes express disappointment, which can make a young athlete feel a lot of pressure.

There is plenty of time to pick your favorite sport and then to focus on it alone. If you are going to be a top athlete in any sport, it will happen no matter what other sports you play. A well-rounded sports background, together with the proper rest, will serve you much better than playing one sport all year round at an early age.

What If I Want To Quit?

If you're playing sports for fun, quitting is probably the last thing on your mind. After all, you're playing sports you enjoy with your friends. You like your coaches, and your parents support you. You're keeping up with your schoolwork, and maybe taking a break here and there when your favorite sports are out of season. No way you would even think about not playing anymore. In fact, sports are something you enjoy as much as or more than anything else you do.

In a perfect world, this is the way it would be for all young athletes. In the real world, however, it is often something different. Some young athletes are finding themselves pushed and pressured into a particular sport. They are told that winning is everything. If they have talent, they are often pressured to specialize in a sport and play it all year round.

This kind of pressure can make a young athlete forget the fun of sports and want to quit.

Anthony D. Meyer, M.D., Clinical Professor and Director of Child & Adolescent Psychiatry at the Medical College of Wisconsin, explains why young children have a difficult time handling too much pressure to excel at sports.

"As pre-teenagers," Dr. Meyer said, "children . . . believe that whatever they do is responsible for what actually happens. If they miss the goal or strike out and the team loses, they believe they are solely at fault. They also have a very, very strong need to please adults, and a coach or parent who feeds into that need may easily push a child beyond his or her breaking point. . . . Some adults will fail to value all aspects of a child's nature and development and focus too heavily on his or her ability to perform certain activities, particularly competitive sports."

This may be a difficult concept for a young athlete to grasp. But it helps to remember sports should be fun. When you first begin to play and pick the sports you like, you should also have a coach who puts the most emphasis on teaching you the skills necessary to play that sport. Winning should not be the main focus. You should not be made to feel you have failed after a loss, or that it was your fault. If a coach or parent tries to make you feel that way, you must understand that they are wrong.

In fact, studies show that most young athletes don't even pay attention to the score. More often, it's the parents who do. If your team loses, but you played your best, that's fine. Don't let losing ruin the fun of learning, competing, and improving. Once

Parents who put pressure on their young athletes usually mean well, but if you feel too much pressure, you can explain to your parents that it is taking away from your enjoyment of your sport.

the fun stops, chances are that you won't want to play for that team anymore, and maybe even quit the sport altogether.

A look at gymnastics gives a perfect example of how sports can be extremely beneficial or potentially harmful to young athletes. The success of teenage gymnasts at the Olympic level makes the sport attractive to young girls. They see Olympic stars like Mary Lou Retton,

Shannon Miller, and Kerri Strug and want to be like them. At the same time, however, there have been reports of young elite gymnasts being pushed beyond their limits, forced to lose weight, and made to practice despite nagging injuries.

But as Dr. Lyle Micheli, the cofounder and director of sports medicine at Boston's Children's Hospital, explained, there are two kinds of gymnastics.

"[There are] the gymnastics at the elite level, in which 200 girls [nationally], at the most, are involved," Dr. Micheli said. "That level contains the vast majority of the reported abuses. Then there is gymnastics for everyone else. [The sport] teaches strength, mobility and flexibility, and balance, and gives a sense of self-worth. I'm behind that kind of gymnastics one hundred percent."

It is a matter of a good way and a bad way to pursue a sport—to have fun as opposed to pushing too hard, too soon. If you decide to try gymnastics, for example, you must have a good coach to teach you the proper techniques. A good coach will bring you along slowly and will not urge you to try difficult maneuvers before you have the skills and abilities to do so. Both you and the coach will enjoy your sessions and you'll feel satisfaction as you begin to improve.

If you feel some aches and pains and want to skip a workout, or several workouts, you must be allowed to do so. If you feel you aren't ready to try a more difficult maneuver, the coach, as well as your parents, should respect your wishes and give you more time. And as you grow and mature, do not let anyone tell you

Gymnastics is often used as an example of a sport in which young girls are pushed beyond what may be good for them physically and mentally. But most young gymnasts enjoy a beneficial, rewarding experience from the sport.

that you are becoming too large or heavy to be a gymnast and need to lose weight. You can always continue with gymnastics for fun, and become more competitive in another sport.

If you began playing your sport for fun, but then find yourself pushed by coaches and parents, you may stop having fun and soon begin to think about quitting. If this happens, try to think of the reasons why you aren't happy. Were you pushed into a sport you didn't really like? Did your coach and/or parents expect too much from you? Did you find it difficult playing a team sport with others? Were you always being told that you did something wrong, made mistakes, or caused your team to lose? And last, but far from least, were you just not having any fun? If your reason for wanting to quit involves your coach, speak to her about it. Or tell your parents the way you feel. If your parents don't understand, try another trusted adult such as a teacher or someone from the clergy.

If you finally decide that you cannot continue with a sport, however, you have a right to leave that sport. What you shouldn't do, however, is think that because one sports experience turned out badly that all sports will be that way. The time may be right to try another sport, not to leave sports completely.

If you had a love of sports when you started, and had fun playing with your friends, you can always find that feeling again, even after a bad experience. To quit entirely, you risk losing all the positive things that participating in sports can give you.

There are many reasons why young athletes quit sports. However, if you choose the right sport or sports from the beginning and keep focused on the fun of sports, there is less of a chance this will happen.

Keep trying new sports and find one or two, or maybe more, that you like. When the time is right, you'll know which sport is your best, how good you can be, and whether you can be a college or professional star, or just someone who plays for exercise, health, and fun. No matter where you wind up, you'll be glad you stuck with it and continued to play.

What Do I Need to Play Certain Sports?

When you start to play sports, you learn the individual skills needed to master each one. At the beginning, try any sport you think you will like. Learn the skills first, see how you do, and then decide if you want to continue with that sport or try another.

Here is a brief summary of some of the skills and physical attributes needed for a number of popular sports. Remember, nothing is absolute. There have been great players in all sports who have surprised a lot of people. They didn't always fit the description of a "typical" athlete in a particular sport. But through hard work and effort, they were able to compete. Don't give up if you feel you don't quite fit the profile.

BASKETBALL This is a sport best played by quick, strong, graceful athletes. The best players can run and jump well. They have good hand-eye coordination to dribble, pass, catch, and shoot the basketball. It takes many hours of practice to learn and perfect these skills. A player must also be able to move quickly and deftly on a relatively small court. It's true that a tall person is always looked upon as a potential basketball player. Tall, average, or short, a player must have the ability to master the skills, run, and jump. The game has a place for everyone who works hard and combines these skills with the desire to excel.

CROSS COUNTRY and **TRACK** If you are a runner, getting better is simply a matter of repetitive practice and natural ability. Runners come in all shapes and sizes. However, sprinters are usually more muscular while distance runners are often very slender. Sprinters must learn to get every ounce of speed out of their bodies in short bursts. Distance runners must combine their speed with great conditioning and mental toughness. There are also specialized track events such as the hurdles, which take skill and timing. Cross-country runners train to go as hard as they can over rough terrain.

FIELD HOCKEY To be a good field hockey player, you must have speed, quickness, and endurance. Much of the game depends on the ability to run, often at full speed. You have to be prepared to run for most of the game, which means being in top shape. You must also learn the skills of handling a small ball with a wooden field-hockey stick. This takes a great deal of practice. Once you learn the basic skills, however, it's just a matter of practicing to become the best player you can be.

GYMNASTICS   A popular sport with young girls, those best suited for gymnastics are small, not too heavy, and very athletic. If you like to tumble and do cartwheels and somersaults, gymnastics might be right for you. You need a good coach to acquire the skills, and cannot be fearful of eventually doing advanced maneuvers that often appear dangerous to those watching.

SOCCER   The requirements for soccer are similar to those for field hockey. As a player, you must have good endurance and be able to run for much of the game. In addition, you must have good coordination to learn the skills of kicking, dribbling, and passing the ball with your feet.

SOFTBALL   Softball (and baseball) players come in all shapes and sizes. They can be small and quick or big and strong. With eight position players and a pitcher, chances are good there will be a place for you. However, you must be able to throw and catch well, learn to field ground balls, and judge popups and fly balls. You must also master one of the most difficult skills in all of sports — hitting a pitched ball with a bat. But even if you don't become a great hitter, you can compensate by becoming a fine fielder or pitcher. There are many ways to help a softball team because so many individual skills are involved. That's why it's a great sport!

SWIMMING   This is a mostly individual sport in which the skills are basic and a great deal of repetition is involved. Top swimmers are usually average height or taller with long arms and legs, which can propel them quickly through the water. A shorter person with shorter arms will have to work harder and use more strokes to cover the same distance in the same time as a taller competitor. Once a swimmer picks a stroke to specialize in (such as the freestyle, breaststroke, backstroke, butterfly, and others), she simply has to practice. She must also learn to dive to start a race and learn how to turn quickly and powerfully when she reaches the end of the pool.

TENNIS Tennis is a sport that requires a variety of skills. Good players are fast and quick and have great hand-eye coordination, as well as the strength to hit the ball hard. A good tennis player must be in top shape

and learn to move in short bursts. Footwork is very important, as is a sense of timing. Tall players might have an advantage serving and having a longer reach when lunging for a ball, but short, quick players can also play well. Tennis is for anyone who takes time to learn the skills and works to become better.

VOLLEYBALL Volleyball is a popular sport that can be loads of fun. The best players are usually tall and quick, and can jump high. This is a sport where the ability to move and jump quickly are extremely important. To do this well, a volleyball player must always be in top physical condition. The skills of serving, setting up, spiking, and blocking are not that difficult to learn. Moving quickly on a relatively small court, a player must have good footwork and be able to communicate verbally with her teammates to avoid collisions and confusion. This is truly a team sport.

There are other sports that have not been covered here. As you can see, most sports are open for just about anyone to try. You might not be perfectly suited to all of them and have some limits as you try to improve. However, you can always try them for fun, and see what you like and where you excel. Then, as you get older, you can choose the sports that are best for you, the ones you enjoy the most and provide you with the most fun and greatest satisfaction.

Always remember one thing: The question "Which sport is right for me?" should be answered *by* you, not *for* you by someone else. This will keep you on the road to being a lifelong athlete and getting all you can out of sports.

Get in the Game!

Learning about sports in general, especially the world of women's sports, will give you even more information as you explore your many options as an athlete. These books and Web sites are a good place to start.

Girl Power on the Playing Field by Andy Steiner (Minneapolis: Lerner, 1999).

Girl to Girl: On Sports by Anne Driscoll (New York: Element, 2000).

Good Sports: Winning, Losing, and Everything in Between by Therese Kauchak (Middleton, WI: American Girl Library, 1999).

Play Like a Girl: A Celebration of Women in Sports edited by Sue Macy and Jane Gottesman (New York: Henry Holt, 1999).

Winning Every Day: Gold Medal Advice for a Happy, Healthy Life! by Shannon Miller and Nancy Ann Richardson (New York: Bantam, 1998).

www.womenssportsfoundation.org
A good, basic site for all you want to know about women in sports.

www.gogirlmag.com
Go, Girl! is a fun, online sports magazine.

www.factmonster.com
Click on "sports" for lots of good information for younger kids, including a section on women's sports.

www.tutornuway.com
Click on "articles," then on "just for athletes" for some valuable sports and sportsmanship information.

Index